VANISHING POINT

Other works by William Trowbridge:

Oldguy: Superhero, 2016
Put This On, Please: New & Selected Poems, 2014
Ship of Fool, 2011
The Packing House Cantata, 2006
The Complete Book of Kong, 2003
The Four Seasons, 2001
Flickers, 2000
O Paradise, 1995
Enter Dark Stranger, 1989
The Book of Kong, 1986

VANISHING POINT

Poems

William Trowbridge

Red Hen Press | *Pasadena, CA*

Book design and layout by Irene Lam
Illustrations by Tim Mayer

Library of Congress Cataloging-in-Publication Data

Names: Trowbridge, William, 1941– author.
Title: Vanishing point : poems / William Trowbridge.
Description: First edition. | Pasadena, CA : Red Hen Press, [2017]
Identifiers: LCCN 2016048364 | ISBN 9781597093651 (pbk. : alk. paper)
Classification: LCC PS3570.R66 A6 2017 | DDC 811/.54—dc23
LC record available at https://lccn.loc.gov/2016048364

The National Endowment for the Arts, the Los Angeles County Arts Commission, the
Dwight Stuart Youth Foundation, the Max Factor Family Foundation, the Pasadena
Tournament of Roses Foundation, the Pasadena Arts & Culture Commission and the
City of Pasadena Cultural Affairs Division, the City of Los Angeles Department of
Cultural Affairs, the Audrey & Sydney Irmas Charitable Foundation, Sony Pictures
Entertainment, Amazon Literary Partnership, and the Sherwood Foundation partially
support Red Hen Press.

First Edition
Published by Red Hen Press
www.redhen.org

ACKNOWLEDGMENTS

Thanks are due to the following publications in whose pages these poems first appeared:

Atlanta Review: "Oldguy: Superhero"; *Boulevard*: "You and Your Shadow"; *Bridge Eight*: "In Memoriam: Spike Jones"; *burntdistrict*: "Elegy," "*Hier Gibt es Blaubeeren*," and "Peony Park, Omaha"; *Chariton Review*: "After Surprising Conversations" and "Mowing"; *Connotation Press*: "Elephant"; *EPOCH*: "Oldguy: Superhero vs. His Nemesis"; *The Georgia Review*: "Where Da Ya Think Yer Goin'"; *The Gettysburg Review*: "Worse Than Useless"; *Green Mountains Review*: "Chain-Link Fence," "It's Good to Be King," "Oldguy: Superhero, Counterterrorist," "Oldguy: Superhero—His Utility Belt," "Oldguy: Superhero, Top Eliminator," "Tilt-A-Whirl," and "The Tooth Fairy"; *I-70 Review*: "Haunted" and "Please, Not That Again"; *Los Angeles Review*: "Caution:"; *Moon City Review*: "I'm Rubber, You're Glue . . ." and "Serendipity"; *Natural Bridge*: "*Gold Diggers of 1933*"; *NEO*: "Peek-A-Boo"; *New Letters*: "Bob Steele," "The Cloakroom," "Fast Forward," "Oldguy: Superhero—His Origin," Oldgiy: Superhero Shuffles Down Memory Lane," "Rainbow Lanes," "Send 25 Cents, Plus 5 Boxtops," "*The Shooter's Bible*," and "Spoilage"; *Paddlefish*: "Old Fools"; *Plainsongs*: "The Alley Kids" and "MiraLAX®"; *Plume*: "Oldguy: Superhero Undercover," "Last Words," "Prizewinner," "Vanishing Point," "Welcome Home," and "Ya Know?"; *Rattle*: "*Battleground*," "Keychain Peep Show," "Oldguy: Superhero, Associate," and "Oldguy: Superhero, Steady Hand"; *River Styx*: "Elisha Cook, Jr." and "Reserve Squad"; *Slant*: "The Hereford Wheel," *South Dakota Review*: "Invasion" and "Long Distance to My Old Coach"; *Sugar House Review*: "Ricochet"; *Tar River Poetry*: "What a Drag It Is Getting Old"; *TriQuarterly*: "Firing the M-1 Garand" and "Moloch Tells All."

Thanks are also due to Charles Harper Webb, Jo McDougall, and Maryfrances Wagner for their invaluable critiques and encouragement, and to David Clewell, rare combination of first-rate poet and eagle-eyed copy editor.

For Thomas Daniel Young

1920–1997

scholar, mentor, friend

CONTENTS

I

II

III

IV

VANISHING POINT

I

TILT-A-WHIRL

It speeds you in a circle on a wavy platform
and, at the same time, whips you around
inside that circle: wheel within a wheel,
to quote Ezekiel. Each year I tried to master
its gyrations, only to regurgitate,
with my corn dog and cherry Coke,
my youthful self-assurance. This dated,
wry contraption, I now read, can be
a model for chaos theory, the spins
of that inner circle erratic as the bully
summoned by some butterfly wing
to beat me up three days in a row
on my way home from school. "Guess,"
he smirked, when I asked why. "I thought
he was a nice man," said killer Perry Smith,
"right up to the minute I cut his throat."
In Italy, a guy was killed by a pig
falling from a balcony two stories up.
Neighbors dined on free ham afterwards.
Some zealot plugs an Austrian archduke,
and the world heaves up eight million corpses.
"Hang on tight," the attendant shouts,
as we brace for gravity's blindside.

WELCOME HOME

Large sign in many American
ports at the end of WW II.

All I have is a black-and-white photo,
taken in our yard, my father holding me,
him still in his khakis, me dwarfed
beneath his service cap, both of us
looking as if the other might bite,
warrior and war baby joined
by biology and chance, him smiling
stiffly for Mother's camera. He brought
souvenirs—his bayonet, a Nazi pistol—
and a taste for Luckies, bourbon,
and rage. When he hugged, his cheek
scraped like sandpaper, how I thought
a hero's face should feel; his slaps
could blur my eyes.

They say three months in combat
fractures a normal mind. He'd spent
almost a year, the details of which
would stay off-limits. We must have
looked like aliens, my mother, sister,
and I, so plump and washed and green,
our neighborhood hospitable as Mars.
"Welcome home," one of the Martians
must have said.

FIRING THE M-1 GARAND

In our backyard, my father,
who never talks about the War,
demonstrates the proper way
to use the sling on the .22 rifle
I bought with my allowance
to play soldier with my pals
in the dump off 95th Street—
cans, bottles, maybe a rat or two.
He winds the strap tightly
around his left arm, puts the butt
up to his shoulder, then raises
the rifle to firing position, keeping,
he notes, the right elbow high,
taking a deep breath, then
holding it. When I try to follow,
he adjusts my elbow, tells me,
"Remember: never aim your rifle,
loaded or not, at anyone you're
not prepared to kill." He lets go
of my arm and, to fill the sudden
hush, adds, "I meant just don't
point guns at people," then turns
and walks quickly away.

BATTLEGROUND

It showed the War was as my father said:
boredom flanked by terror, a matter of keeping
low and not freezing. "You wore your helmet

square," he said, not "at some stupid angle,
like that draft-dodger Wayne," who died
so photogenically in *The Sands of Iwo Jima*.

Those nights I heard shouts from the dark
of my parents' room, he was back down
in his foxhole, barking orders, taking fire

that followed him from France and Germany,
then slipped into the house, where it hunkered
in the rafters and thrived on ambush. We kept

our helmets on, my mother and I,
but there was no cover, and our helmets
always tilted. He'd lump us with the ones

he called "JohnDoes," lazy, stupid, useless.
We needed to straighten up and fly right,
pick it up, chop chop, not get "nervous

in the service." We'd duck down like GIs
where German snipers might be crouched
in haylofts, their breaths held for the clean shot.

"Bang," my father said, "the dead went down,
some like dying swans, some like puppets
with their strings cut." I wanted to hear more,

but he'd change the subject, talk about
the pennant, the Cards' shaky odds, how Musial
was worth the whole JohnDoe lot of them.

'49 BUICK

It was parked outside my father's office
at the Wilson Packing House, with me, age seven,
and my mother inside. A strike was on,

and my father, plant manager, said pickets
had shot out windows and bombed homes,
that our house, in the suburbs, could be next.

So he had us wait for him all day in the Buick,
a new straight-8 Super, where he and guards
the company hired could see us. Dad said

the union was communist-run and the police,
there to control the strikers, might as well be
painted on posts. This was South Omaha,

he said, all d.p.'s: Polacks, Bohunks, including
the police. They had nasty habits and bred
like insects. He brought his service .45 to work

each day of that sweltering summer, before
most cars had AC. I was bored instead of
frightened, since the Buick felt sturdy as a fort

and guards watched nearby. Mother played the radio
—mostly music and news, but one day it aired
a dramatized short story titled "Leiningen

Versus the Ants," starring basso William Conrad
as a settler whose plantation in Brazil is attacked
by thumb-sized killer ants in a swarm two miles wide

and ten miles long. It chilled me, sweating
in the back seat with my comics and bubble gum
as the hours plodded. Dozing, I dreamed that

Polacks, Bohunks, and fanged ants—Reds every one
—swarmed from their Slavic nests to our west-side
cul-de-sac, made bridges of themselves to stretch

across the moat we'd built, devouring neighbors
down to white bone, chewing into our Buick,
laying eggs. When a thorny feeler touched my leg,

I kicked awake and looked around, glad to see
my mother and the company shield, safe again
inside our shiny Buick, inside 1949.

HAUNTED

Back then in Omaha, *The Rosary Hour*
came into my bedroom after school,
on my Philco, following *Polka Party*—

The Six Fat Dutchmen, Frankie Yankovic,
Jimmy Sturr, Whoopee John, then
ghostly chants about "the hour of our

death" repeated non-stop and in
a dreadful rush. I felt the programs
were connected (Poles were Catholics,

weren't they?)—"mother of God"
and "she's too fat for me." "Blessed
art thou" and "that oom-pa-pa."

I couldn't pull my dizzy mind away.
My folks were Presbyterians, whatever
that meant. I was a Balsa Modelist

soon to convert to Plastic, though
I knew of poor St. Vitus, surmised
he was the martyrs' polka king.

THE ALLEY KIDS

Mother told me to come in when they
appeared, shaggy among hollyhocks

that grew thick as jungle verdure
behind our backyard—Indian territory,

the other side of the DMZ, sheer drop
off the edge of our squared little planet.

They were all related, the story went,
nearly interchangeable, spawned

from some wooly gene pool. The meanest
had a club foot and once punched me

breathless after school. Why were they
so hurtful? Dad said they had nothing

else to do. They needed a good, hard
scrubbing, a lesson in right manners,

shop class. Then they could slough off
alley ways, go out for sports. Play ball.

THE TOOTH FAIRY

I pictured a figure somewhere between Tinker Bell
and Dopey, wafting down through slumberland
to collect, for some uncanny reason, my latest molar,
placed with care between sheet and pillow, where,
in the morning, I'd find another shiny dime. The fairy
hailed, I felt, from the box-top capital, Battle Creek,
Michigan, where wizards conjured up the Quaker
puffed-oat-shooting cannon ring and the Lone Ranger
eight-color-lens signal light and six-shooter, stashed
under my blanket after bedtime. Who could doubt
the gospel of magic, with the evidence so clear?

"Ask the tooth fairy," I overheard my dad snap back
one day when Mother said she wanted a new washer.
"Go tell the tooth fairy, you little fruit," said the bully,
when he took my ring and pistol after show-and-tell.

THE CLOAKROOM

is what they called it, though in third grade,
the only ones we knew wore cloaks were Goldilocks
and Dracula. In winter, it smelled of dank wool,

sweat, must, the floor lumpy with wet galoshes.
It could get close in the cloakroom and go black
when both doors closed. We learned that

"cloak" meant what it did: cloaked in shame
the ones who misbehaved and earned an hour
in its darkness. Ruthie, from St. Cecilia's, said

the nuns would make you kneel there with your
bare knees on raw rice till you whined out
25 Hail Marys. Someone told her they smelled

brimstone. We heard that Sally Bliss let Bob Malone
feel her up there during recess. She got renamed
"Cloakroom Sally." In my cloakroom dream,

she came in and closed the doors. But we slipped
on the rice, fell to our knees, and as kernels gnawed,
galoshes exhaled brimstone, there in the wooly dark.

KEYCHAIN PEEP SHOW

I found it in my parents' room,
center-bottom dresser drawer,
beneath the socks: a little plastic scope
with a naked woman posed inside,

breasts uplifted, red hair flowing down,
a globe balanced on one shoulder,
like Atlas in my *Classic Comics* book
and seeming from that netherworld.

I peeped and peeped again, felt brash
as Peeping Tom, who eyed Godiva's
plenty as she rode through Coventry,
past discreetly shuttered windows;

randy as the lecher leering
at his master's wife undressing
in the nickel peep-show classic
What the Butler Saw; licentious

as those elders ogling Susanna
at her bath among the honeysuckle.
But I felt more like Howard Carter
at his first peep through the door

to Tutankhamun's shadowed chambers
when asked if there was anything
inside to see. "Yes," he said.
"Wonderful things."

CHAIN-LINK FENCE

Exterminate the brutes!
—Mr. Kurtz

I recall the loud *chink* it makes when
a foul ball hits, much like those the head
of my fourth-grade classmate Terry made
when our gym teacher had enough
of his antics during recess. Terry and a pal

had formed The Mummy Club, reason
for them to shout and whisper "Mummy"
through the school day. *Chink, chink, chink,*
went his head. "Mum-mum-mummy!"
he cried back, "Mum-mum-mummy!"

while the rest of us stood by. Glad enough
it wasn't us, we kept the whole thing quiet,
me for more than 60 years now.
The teacher may be long dead, a guy
for whom I lately have more sympathy,

like when some punk drives up behind me
at a stoplight with his woofer buffeting
my rib cage. *Chink, chink, chink,*
I'd love to show him. "Mum-mum-mummy!"
answers memory, voice young as yesterday.

RESERVE SQUAD

Thank God for the athletes and their rejection.
Without them, there would have been no emotional
need, and . . . I'd be a crackerjack salesman
in the garment district.
　　　　—Mel Brooks

Reserved for what? we asked ourselves
—the four-eyed, the clumsy, the pint-sized,
ungainly in cleats and shoulder pads,
left to tape on the droopy pants stretched
out and discarded by first-string
guards and tackles, who turned us into
blocking dummies, knocking us carp-eyed,
drawing blood. For games, we got plain
helmets and nameless jerseys. Cheerleaders,
high-kicking, sang out the age-old promise
to the victors: "First and ten! Do it again!"

We didn't think they sang for us,
Prufrock jocks, benched for the season,
unlisted in the program, offside, out
of bounds, intentionally grounded
in the pinched and fleeting realm
of prom king and homecoming queen,
till graduation, when we stood up,
and it was first and ten, reserves.

BOB STEELE

1907–1988

He rode out of our Zenith after school,
in black-and-white days filled
with antique oaters starring Hoppy,
Lash, Roy, Tex, all hailing from when
Republic Pictures cranked out 50 B-flicks
of The Three Mesquiteers. Bob,
worth the other two and all the rest,
was "Tucson Smith" in *Lone Star Raiders*,
Pals of the Pecos, *Shadows on the Sage*.
Saddlemates, *Riders of the Rio Grande*
—where hats were black or white
and goodness could drop villainy
with a Colt .44 from half a mile away.

Work-clad, lean, taciturn, and, yes,
steely-eyed, maybe a little on the short side,
he showed the rules for manhood: shoot
straight, ride like a Mongol archer,
call women "Ma'am," don't croon
like Gene or swagger like the Duke.

When he traded his six guns for a gat
in *The Big Sleep*, he could have won
a staring match with Bogie if the script
had given him a shot. You could buy
Bob Steele comics in the Fifties. After that

the parts got smaller and his dark hair
whiter, till he wound up playing geezers:
"Trooper Duffy" on *F Troop*, and last,
"Charlie" in *Nightmare Honeymoon*.

A footnote now, he filled theaters
on weekends before the War, and
on school-day afternoons, his walloping
posse from Generation Picture Tube.
Bob Steele, as the script must read,
grew old, then died, but, saddlemates,
you should have seen him ride.

MEADOWLARK

1932–2015

For me, [the best basketball player I've
ever seen] would be Meadowlark Lemon.
—Wilt Chamberlain

He played the 'Trotters'
jolly trickster,

brought guffaws when,
all grins, he'd stash

the ball beneath his jersey,
flip it behind

his always-baffled,
mostly-white opponents

(the Washington Generals,
record 1 and 1600+)

or whip his half-court
hook-shot up and in,

then flit off
to steal another pass.

He charmed the haters,
broganed or silk-tied,

who took him for just
another dancing coon,

slapping their knees,
getting their rocks off

as he doused them
with that bucket of confetti

and piped their children
into practicing his moves.

PREFACE TO UNLYRICAL BALLADS

The Johnson Smith & Co. Catalogue:
Surprising Novelties, Puzzles, Tricks,
Joke Goods, Useful Articles, Etc.

Give me The Ventrillo, to throw my voice
across the room and amaze my friends
—or foes. *The Genuine Mediumship Handbook*,
by Swami Bhakta Vishita, could activate
my psychic powers, bolstered further by
Black Art, *Practical Hypnotism*, *Napoleon's*
Oraculum and Book of Fate, *The Mysteries of*
Clairvoyance, and *How to Woo*. For partying,
there's the Dribble Glass, Electric Squirt
Button, Loaded Cigarettes, Joy Buzzer, or
Ring with Sponge ("Shake Hands, Then???").
Whoops, did you just plant your buns on my
Whoopee Cushion? Who cut the cheese??
Or maybe I'll master sleight of hand with my
Mephisto Changing Cards, Multiplying
Ball, Siberian Chain Escape, Bewildering
Blocks, or Conjurer's Extra Finger. Whoa:
mess with me, and you'd get a taste of my
Spring Steel Patent Telescopic Police Club,
or maybe you'd rather face my Vest Pocket
Young America Safety-Hammer Revolver,
("Also Excellent for Ladies") or the Ejector
Model Baby Hammerless Revolver ("Only
4 ¼ Inches"), Tear Gas Fountain Pen Pistol,

or, if adaptability's called for, my Potato Pistol
("Uses Ordinary Potatoes for Ammunition").
And try to find me if I don the Nu-Face Mask,
Huge Lips, Exaggeroscope Spectacles,
Bleeding Ear and Nose Bandages. If I feel
musical, there's The Magic Nose Flute, Baby
Jazz Kazoo Saxophone ("You Can Play It If
You Can Talk"), Mignon Concert Fairy Chimes,
Musical Canary, Chromatic Rolmonica
("No Practice Necessary"), Celestaphone
("Latest and Best of All Stringed Instruments"),
or Base Ball Club Band Mouth Organ. If art
and science fail, I could pack my Gladstone Bag
and employ *600 Ways to Get Rich* to corner
the market on digestive pills, vinegar, metal
cement, rat killer, shaving paste, foot ointment,
hair dye, or "essences, etc., etc., etc." I owe you,
Mr. Smith, for triggering that first spontaneous
overflow of Confetti Grenades, recollected in
what might pass for tranquility—if I could silence
the Pocket Cat Cries and Surprise Torpedo Whistles.

PLEASE, NOT THAT AGAIN

How burdensome they seemed, wartime
oldies that could drive our parents teary:

"I'll Be Seeing You," with its hint
of being swept off in a global riptide;

or the shaky follow-up of "I'll Be Home
for Christmas," followed by a shakier

"Don't Sit Under the Apple Tree
(with Anyone Else But Me)," "Comin'

In on a Wing and a Prayer," or "Ac-
Cent-Tchu-Ate the Positive." We suffered

them on the old cathedral radio, crooned
by Crosby and Sinatra, had to watch them

strangled on *The Lawrence Welk Show*
or laced with Como's heavy dose

of sedative. Dad told us, "Straighten Up
and Fly Right," Mom hummed, "Keep

the Home Fires Burning"—till our music
cut the cord. Brash and free of corn,

it hailed rock 'n' roll, caught Maybellene
at the top of the hill, moaned "m' baby-doll,

m' baby-doll, m' baby-doll." We played it
loud and often, but they never understood.

PEONY PARK, OMAHA

I got my first job there, where everyone in Omaha
came to cool off in the summer—four-million-gallon pool,
like a small lake with a beach, high board, high tower,
plus indoor and outdoor ballrooms for the bands
coming through: Ellington, Kenton, Basie, Herman.
I flipped burgers in the refreshment stand, 85¢ an hour,
and mopped up after closing. Once a week, I helped
scoop back sand that had worked its way onto the bottom.
If we didn't, the water would look dirty. Every time,
we'd pull in an adult-sized turd or two. Blacks
were barred, since they were said to be unclean.
There were drownings and dumb accidents: a guy dove
off the tower with a swim mask on, which splintered
into his face. The 16 lifeguards for the 4th were too few
for the dead kid. Our crew ogled the girls in swimsuits,
how they'd reach down and tuck a shapely cheek
back under cover. The jockeys showed up Mondays,
horny little guys who carried knives and grudges.
When we got bored, which was frequently, we'd
mold ten pounds of burger into a meat-puppet head
and, from behind the grill partition, work its mouth
to rattle customers. Once, we tossed a handful into the fan
by the jukebox, where the ducktailers liked to preen.
They'd played "Transfusion," by Nervous Norvus, 15 times.
They didn't dare retaliate, since our crew included four
bruisers who doubled as goon squad, hired to bum's-rush
troublemakers out the front gate. We held our own Olympics,

with events like who could carry the most cases of beer
up from the cellar at once (the goon squad always
took gold) or who could get the most burgers on the grill
at once. I broke the record with 120, scorched down
to silver-dollar size. In later years, the crowds kept shrinking,
even after blacks were allowed to swim. After the bankruptcy,
developers razed the place and built a mini-mall, leaving
half the front gate as "memento." But there's still
a Facebook page. Old-timers will tell you, tears welling,
how they grew up with the place—white ones, that is.

INVASION

Omaha, January 1958

Watch the skies, everywhere, keep looking!
Keep watching the skies!
　　　　—closure to *The Thing from Another World*

We heard it on the PA, second period:
three bodies found in a shack in Lincoln,
a couple and their daughter, age two, shot,

it seemed, by the older daughter's boyfriend,
Charles Starkweather, the child's body
stuffed into an outdoor privy. Another murder

was announced after math, and two more
during study hall, the killer and the girlfriend
said to be heading up toward us. What

could they want? There was an APB.
Radios chattered, like we'd imagined
if the Russians finally struck, when the EBS

would tell us, "This is not a drill,"
as SAC bombers, kept ready out at Offutt,
lifted into WW III. In Lincoln, the police chief

told citizens, "Arm yourselves!" like in *Invasion
of the Body Snatchers*, parka-ed vigilantes
in the backs of pickups, prowling neighborhoods

for aliens. We imagined Starkweather's eyes
—unearthly, staring above a .38 or 12 gauge. What
would we do? We were frightened and lighthearted

as the teens who sounded the early warning
in *The Blob*. Our parents came to drive us home,
cars lining the street beside our high school.

We heard sirens on 72nd, saw police,
weapons drawn, storm Ryan's Junk Yard
on a false tip. But maybe he had arrived,

a thought that caromed through the state,
where the couple was seen in eight towns
simultaneously. We felt surrounded. Mother,

eyes raised, asked God if anyone was safe
anymore. Dad loaded up his service .45
and scanned the TV news. "Duck and cover"

couldn't have saved those kids from Bennett,
found dumped in a storm cellar,
or the human noshes in *Night of the Living Dead*.

Three more dead, back in Lincoln,
said the news, as I watched cars pass our house,
one with a couple in it, moving slow. Too slow.

Nothing happened. A few days later,
they were caught: Starkweather, ex-garbage-man,
stubby and bowlegged, who tried to comb his hair

like James Dean's, and his mousy girlfriend,
Caril Ann, 14, in cowgirl boots, who swore
she'd been a hostage. They looked haggard,

unexceptional, had surrendered meekly.
Life went back to normal: routine, secure.
Undeceived, we continued keeping watch.

HAIR

We wore crewcuts.
They wore ducktails.

We wore flattops.
They wore waterfalls.

We wore Princetons.
They wore Detroits,
spit curls, conks,
pompadours with "breakers."

We used Butch Wax, Lucky Tiger.
They used Blue Magic.
Royal Crown, congolene.

We drank Coke and Pepsi.
They drank Lucky Tiger.

SPOILAGE

When the can company switched me to working
near the heavy presses, my ears rang all the time,
a high-pitched dial tone. Their doctor said
that was normal, not to expect workman's comp

or time off. The company didn't offer earplugs,
and we were too stupid or heedless to buy them.
No safety gloves either, for those who had to
handle tin plate that whipped out razor sharp.

One guy took a week to get stitched up,
his hand like a job by Dr. Frankenstein.
They gave us 15-minute breaks twice a day,
but the union steward said, "Don't let me

see your ass back here inside 45." I ate lunch
from the machines: the cafeteria food stank
like soup-kitchen leftovers. An efficiency expert
said to speed the lines way up, which made

some of us go haywire now and then, driving
forklifts into walls, shoving screwdrivers into cogs
that moved the conveyer belts. "Brrrr-reakdown!"
somebody'd whoop, to a wave of cheers. One day

I shoved a hand truck into a 10-foot stack
of gallon oil cans, watched them crunch in,
topple, and gimp across the floor like busted
wind-up toys: *Havoline Motor . . . Keeps Your*

Engine. . . . Mike Reid, our asshole foreman,
would try to get you fired for stuff like that
or if you worked too slow. But the building
took up a city block, so there were lots of places

out of sight. Anyway, we weren't surprised
to read about some guy showing up somewhere
to work one day and shooting every white shirt
he could find. Halfway into my second summer,

the company sent us letters saying they'd had
$100,000 worth of "spoilage" so far that year,
and would we please "help our team get
back on track." Then came another letter,

asking us to consider buying stock, to boost
our "sense of ownership." No shit: "ownership."

RAINBOW LANES

—Open All Night—

was across the street, where we went sometimes
when the can company stuck us four packers
on the redeye shift, the lines shut down,
cleanup taking a couple of hours. Why they
gave us eight, we didn't know or care, at work
in what felt like a five-story cargo barge drifting
in deep space, radios dead. When he ran out
of busy-work ideas, Mo, the foreman, whom
everybody liked, would say, "Don't let me
see you sorry bastards till quitting time."

Driving home seemed too far, too risky,
though bowling then was a knee-deep slog
through sleeplessness and boredom. The place
had 30 lanes, a long bar, and an arcade room,
with only us and some neighborhood strays,
junkies, maybe, sweating delivery. Rental shoes
stank of Desenex, mold, and cigarette butts.
The whole place did. You could get a burger
sealed in cellophane from a rattly machine
you had to pound on. A Pabst cost six bits.
We'd go three rounds, or four. Who counts?

Harvey, a league guy, always won. Now
and then, one of us got pissed enough
at his yet-another-strike dance to start
a little pushy-shovey, which always ended

in a grudging handshake. Mostly no one
gave a shit. We'd try trick shots: blind man,
backward between the legs, Kamikaze.
By sunrise, we'd go back and doze
in empty boxcars, waiting to punch out.

I'M RUBBER, YOU'RE GLUE . . .

In third grade, after an all-school convocation,
we saw the puddle in the contoured chair seat,
left by Dorothy Smith, whose name I've changed.

She'd been escorted out like someone
crippled, bereaved, or contagious. Maybe
she was ill, but I, who barely knew her,

turned her into those soppy pants, coining
"Damp Dorothy," which stuck and made her cry,
grade-school miniature of "Wrong Way" Riegels,

whose Rose Bowl blunder lost the game
for Cal, or Ethelred "the Unready," doomed
to be the comic note in the *Doomsday Book*,

not to mention Slovenia's Vinko Bogataj,
Mr. "Agony-of-Defeat," whose mega-ski-crash
opened *Wide World of Sports* each Sunday

for two decades. May Dorothy's trial have turned,
somehow by now, sweet as Vinko's, whose fall
bought a ticket to America for a week

of *Wide World's* 20ᵗʰ jubilee—Ali asking
for his autograph. I like to see it this way:
after high school, Dorothy, alone at a party,

on her third Black Russian, recounts
the seat-puddle mishap, and the little jerk
who nicknamed her, ending with a quiet laugh

that charms a charming guy so much
they end up married in a neighborhood where
she's treasured as just plain, well, Dorothy.

THE HARVARD CLASSICS

My grandfather bought a set for his living room,
51 imitation-leather-bound volumes billed

by Collier & Son as a liberal education distilled
to "a five-foot shelf." He was a university dean—

OK, of agriculture—but they looked like something
from bookshelves in films about the highborn,

had that air of seasoned privilege, of greenswards,
laced with groundskeepers, footmen, upstairs maids.

When Grandpa died, my father, who didn't read
books, moved them to our living room, said they

showed class, taste, education. The room tried on
their eminence, became a trifle less unHarvard.

One afternoon, intrigued, I pulled out Volume 4,
Complete Poems in English, Milton, whose sermonics

in thundering blank verse dismissed me back
to my shelf of *Classic Comics*. Ten years later,

the books languished in a yard sale, marked down
with their kind in yards across the country.

II

VANISHING POINT

It was her voice that made
the sky acutest at its vanishing.
—"The Idea of Order at Key West"

I learned it in art class, second grade,
how to make my crayon portraits
of our house, posted by Mother
on the fridge, look more real; how
the nearest corner of a square looks
taller than the farther ones, how
two parallel lines begin converging
as the distance grows, till they
vanish into the horizon, which
changes as we turn inside the cone
of our cognition, which moves
each time we move, like Harpo
mirroring Groucho in *Duck Soup*.

It smacks of Plato's cave, this mortal
dunce cap that shapes the world
for us, keeps our cares life-sized
and shrinks to indefinite the faraway,
like Wounded Knee or Auschwitz
or those figures keening in the streets
and deserts on our living-room TV.

IT'S GOOD TO BE KING

if they call you Richard the Lionhearted,
honcho of the Crusades and hero to Robin Hood;
or The Sun King, Louie, who fought three wars
and made France the toughest thug in Europe;
or maybe even The Magnanimous, like Alfonso
of Aragon, though you'd be among eight others,
along with seven The Conquerors, eleven The Goods,
and thirteen The Wises, suggesting subjects had
better things to do than think up kingly handles,
further shown in Serbia, where ten were dubbed
a worn and noncommittal The Crowned.

For dark-siders, there's The Impaler, Vlad III
of Wallachia, known to us as Dracula, (followed
diminutively by Basarab IV, The Little Impaler).
Then there's The Madman, Scotland's Donald II,
or, for those who want to specialize, Norway's
Eric II, The Priest Hater, or Basil II of Byzantium,
The Bulgar Slayer. The Cruel's comprehensive,
if you don't mind bunking with four others. Ditto
with The Hammer and—ho hum—The Terrible.

But even if you have to share, it's pretty good
to be king, unless as with Ethelred, subjects
turn wiseass and label you "The Unready."
Or consider Pamplona's García IV, The Trembling,
or England's James II, The Be-shitten. And how about

Normandy's Robert II, The Curthose, or Magnus II,
The Barn-lock, or Byzantium's Michael IV, The Minus-
a-Quarter (of what?), or Michael V, The Caulker.

Buck past those and, in the next roundup,
you might get branded The Accursed, The Gouty,
The Clubfoot, The Sluggard, The Stammerer,
The Impotent, The Who Fights Alone, The Careless,
The Elbow-High, The Dung-Named, The Bad,
(though that could be good), The Unavoidable,
The From Overseas, The Hare Foot, The Spider,
The Stuttering and Lame, or The Posthumous.

Still, it's good to be king. You're the law,
and the flings and snappy outfits can't be beat.
But make me Portugal's Sancho I, The Populator;
please, not Evailo of Bulgaria, The Cabbage.

WHERE DA YA THINK YER GOIN'

The adder-faced hired gun in *Shane*,
Palance—lanky, black-clad, spoiling
for an unfair fight—leans back
against the saloon porch wall,
barracuda waiting for a little fish.
His visage on an arsenic bottle
could alert the legally blind
from five feet off. Dogs slink away
from his shadow. Animals know.

                                    Enter
a feisty little sodbuster, in town
for some redeye. "Hey, cummeer,"
says Palance, ambling toward him,
smiling, thumbs hooked on gun belt,
"Where da ya think yer goin',"
he says, sitting back on a barrel rim.
The sodbuster moves toward the saloon.
Palance moves with him, blocking
the doors, putting on one black glove,
thunder in the background.

                                    Who
wouldn't want to be news that bad,
to say those words, when the bozo
in the red Ram cuts us off, or better yet,
when the white-collar thief prepares
to launder another million or when
the torturer makes his merry way to work:

"Where da ya think yer goin'."

                                                                        But
the sodbuster likely fits us better,
stepping in a mud puddle, looking up
from street level to try to match
the death's-head stare of the goon
the money's backing—we, too, left
to face the sudden barrel of his .44,
our heirloom fly-apart not halfway
clear of our holster.

MOLOCH TELLS ALL

OK, I've got this thing about money, wanting
lots of it—no, all. So it was the shits, flapping

around God like some nutso canary, cooing
Holy, Holy, Holy 24/7. But

after I joined the big rebellion, I had to
raise this issue: the Big Guy's ALL-powerful,

so whatever ordinance we use, we end up
clusterfucked. "You think too much," they said.

And, boom, welcome to Hell. Then Lucifer,
now Satan, starts this Chamber of Commerce

spiel about making a heaven of Hell. Great,
and let's go buy some Gobi oceanfront.

But actually, Hell didn't turn out bad at all,
God seeming to forget that "seraphim" means

"the burning ones." We're almost pure fire,
so it was like Br'er Fox tossing Br'er Rabbit

into the briar patch. "Ooo! Ow! Please,
no more!" we hollered, exchanging high-fives.

It's great to be top dog in the avarice game.
Right now I'm into pyramids and hedge funds,

but I'm framing up a sure-fire deal I'd like you
to look over after I help schlep another batch

of groans and gnashings up to His Grovelship.
We can whipsaw Satan and his Bozos, rule

the board from Boardwalk, and charge fiendish rent
wherever they park their incandescent asses.

RICOCHET

Copied from the '40s oaters we watched
on TV every school-day afternoon,
it was our favorite sound to make when
we played cowboys, cops, or soldiers:

P-tang! Poot-a-ping! "Missed me, kraut!"
In our games, all ricochets were misses,
which wasn't true for the shirtless guy
in Minneapolis I saw brought down by

a warning shot police fired as he bolted
down an alley. Never shoot at a flat,
hard surface, say the safety manuals,
advice too late for me when my BB

caromed back and hit my eyelid or when
a cue ball took me for the corner pocket
or for Israel Torres, who, while flaunting
for his girlfriend, turned bull's-eye for his

own pistol shot. *Galatians 6:7* preaches,
"For whatever a man soweth. . . ." You
know the rest, as you also know what
"comes around"—rules that often hold

for us but not for the big-time bullies,
thieves, and liars, who seem protected
by our childhood rules. *P-tang! Twee!
Pa-ting!* "Missed us again, patsies."

PRIZEWINNER

I answer the door and find a large crowd,
    some men in suits in front saying they're
        happy to present me with a giant check.

From the *Reader's Digest* Sweepstakes?
    Fantasy Football? The Lottery? Wimbledon?
        I don't remember entering any of those,

but the giant check's for serious money—oodles
    of zeros—and they say Price Waterhouse
        certifies there can be no error. The press,

dangling boom mikes, asks how I
    feel about my giant check. Pretty good,
        I tell them. When everybody leaves, I try

to get the giant check into my car, so I can
    deposit it in my small bank account. But I drive
        a Beetle, and the giant check won't

fold up. I have to rent a U-Haul van.
    When I get to my bank, the teller says,
        sorry, they don't cash giant checks.

The manager confirms this, giving me
    a suspicious look. So I wrestle the giant check,
        which feels like it's gotten bigger,

back into the van and drive to a larger bank,
    where I'm told they've received an alert
        from the smaller bank and have

rung for the authorities. When police arrive,
    they ask why I just happen to be carrying
        a giant check around town, acting la-de-da

like I think they're maybe blind or stupid.
    They ask if I realize that giant checks
        could be used by Moslemites to undermine

our nation's economy, that check paper
    can be converted into weapons. They say
        I could be a Moslemite, though

my shoes look Jewboy. The bomb squad
    screeches up and pitches the giant check
        into the street, where they try to detonate it,

using a midget robot to probe the perimeter.
    When I tell them it's not a bomb, they look
        nonplussed, then bring out

flamethrowers, turning the giant check
    into ash. "Watch your head," says a cop
        as he shoves me into the squad car.

SMILE

"You'll find that life is still worthwhile,"
    sang Nat King Cole, "if you just smile."
        It starts when you're a baby, just

a twitch at first. But soon, picked up
    without a lesson, it signals pleasure,
        love, contentment, mirth.

But a Frenchman found it must
    involve the eyes if it isn't shallow
        as that yellow Walmart button's.

He named the real thing, of course,
    after himself—the Duchenne Smile,
        distinct from the Glasgow Smile,

which that city's razor gangs, who
    once were babies, too, devised:
        slit both sides of the quarry's mouth

and beat or stab till facial muscles
    clench to rip a bloody smile
        from ear to ear—like someone might

deface a happy poster. The actor
    Tommy Flanagan got his outside
        a nightclub in that city; Elizabeth Short,

nicknamed the "Black Dahlia," found
   halved in an LA vacant lot, got one
      from her mystery maimer; The Joker

can thank his dad ("Let's put a smile
   on that face.") for his—though all were
      Duchenne-smiling babies once, as were

the death-metal rockers Glasgow Smile,
   whose album features "Retched One"
      and "Man's Disease."

GOLD DIGGERS OF 1933

The women who want a showbiz job
instead of marriage are the "gold diggers"
in this Depression comedy that starts

with a pre-code Busby Berkeley take
on "We're in the Money," showing enough
sassy flesh to re-energize the censors,

the girls looking how you can't imagine
your grandma would have looked
had she been among them, kicking up

their heels, counterpoint to the boys
goose-stepping through Berlin
and Munich, who later, off in Poland,

will dig their gold from human molars
and give a new twist to "concentration,"
though now the Nazi nights are rife

with giddy marchers in formations—
phalanx, rune, swastika, moving
in torchlight on a *Seig heil!* tidal wave—

inversion of the Berkeley numbers, whose girls
combine their amplitude into posies,
violins, and Deco wedding cakes. In Germany,

the beauty Irma Grese, then 10, who dreams
of movie stardom, will later get an SS job
and earn fame as "The Beast of Belsen."

HIER GIBT ES BLAUBEEREN

(HERE THERE ARE BBUEBERRIES)

caption on photos of SS women auxiliaries
being served blueberries on a July 22, 1944
day-trip to Solahütte, recreation center for
staff at Auschwitz-Birkenau, 18 miles away.

The women perch, like birds, along a deck rail:
Mmmm, good, they mime, giggling as they
ham it up behind big spoonfuls, some with mouths
agape, nestling style, while a demure civilian
accordionist pumps out Nordic forest hymns.

But it's not all fun in this photo-story, which turns
like a children's homily. In the last shot, the berries
are all eaten, shown by the women, who hold out
empty bowls. Some look wistful, others mock tears,
all having been such greedy little birds.

GOOD-BYE, ANGEL OF DEATH

on the 1992 verification of the death of Nazi doctor
Josef Mengele, "The Angel of Death"—by matching
DNA samples from the blood of his son Rolfe with
those from remains found buried outside São Paulo.

We could forget the tabloids' boldface whispers
of a hatchery for Hitler clones in São Paulo
or meat lockers packed with Aryan louts
cryogenized for their Führer's second coming,
schemes said to be concocted in the brainpan
of that skull we found, matched half and half
in the forensic photo with the tautly grinning
flesh from 1944. But how confidently he stares
from either side, the eyeball and the empty socket,
as if we just stepped off the train at Birkenau.

SEND 25 CENTS, PLUS 5 BOXTOPS

Not from Oz or Never-Never Land,
this was real-world: Battle Creek,

Michigan, the source—the first mail
I got that wasn't a birthday card

from Grandma or a year's subscription
to *Boy's Life*, picked by Uncle Al. There,

in our mailbox: a brown-paper package
ordered by me, delivered to my four-block

universe, after my reverse-fast on five
lousy boxes of Kix and a month-long vigil.

Inside, the Lone Ranger Atomic Bomb ring—
exact replica, I was sure, of the one

that won the War. The bomb was silver
with a red tail, on a gold-looking ring

with eagle wings on top. You could
pull it off the ring and drop it

from your model B-29 on Japs, with their
buckteeth and squinty eyes, hiding

in the shag. You could make an A-bomb sound
—*KA-BLAM!*—when it hit, picture the glowing

whoosh of mushroom cloud as playmates
vied to give the coolest death-cries.

DOWN AT THE END OF LONELY STREET

Did it unfold like a daily double, an easy
lay, Irresistible Grace? One minute cruising
drive-ins, the next crossed over into Sun,
proclaimed surprise pharaoh—a redneck kid
who had the "nigger sound," the whine, the hips,
somehow just what the swelling market of his classmates
had to have: "ELVIS!" we sobbed, and Graceland
rose, its basement oozing Cadillacs.

He must have marveled for a while, like any teen
with 90 grand in checking, though later
he looked like someone sweating hard to charm
a loan shark come for teeth and knees.

WHITEOUT

In 1845, Rear Admiral Sir John Franklin and a crew
of 124 embarked on a fatal voyage to find the Northwest
Passage. On word of their failure and death, England still
hailed Franklin as a hero of the Empire.

For fear of succumbing to the ways
of savages, the officers eschewed

blubber for tinned meats that leaked
lead from the seams, refused parkas,

choosing flannel coats that got soaked,
then froze. They turned their backs

on dogsleds and igloos, which also stank
of "going native"—something their store

of Bibles, novels, carpet slippers,
silverware, and button polishers

assuredly did not. Finally, in place
of blubber, protection from the scurvy

that wracked their bones, the still-living—
snow-blind and starving, their ship

bound fast in Arctic ice—gallantly
ate the dead till the last survivor froze.

IN MEMORIAM: SPIKE JONES

1911–1965

Needle for pomposity's balloon,
banana peel for the jackboot, he spiked
decorum's fruit punch with a double dose
of fire alarms, gunshots, Bronx cheers,
slide whistles, grunts, snorts, and sneezes.

In bow tie and big-squares suit
with bigger shoulders, he slammed
"Cocktails for Two" into hyperdrive,
sloshed gasoline on "My Old Flame,"
brought the trauma out in "Liebestraum":

"My clinging vine, my voice for thee
doth whine, love; you're older than
Auld Lang Syne," set to banjo, flute,
hiccup, washboard, and snore,
with refrain of "B.O. Rinso WHITE!"

I memorized my favorite parts, set
my fellow miscreants giggling behind
the Teutonic back of old Miss Brendt,
her hair blue and furious. Afterwards,
I'd flash the V, pretending I was there

when Spike's "Der Führer's Face"
sent "Deutschland Über Alles" under:
"Not to love der Führer is a great
disgrace, so vee Heil—*blat*—Heil—
blat—right in der Führer's face."

THE SHOOTER'S BIBLE

The World's Best-Selling Firearms Reference

My schoolboy pals and I studied it like seminarians
do the Scriptures, each page an argument for faith
in beauty males could talk about. We thumbed

through Colts, Berettas, Mausers, Kalashnikovs,
Uzis—the world rendered in small-arms—
and, outshining all, the Rigby .600 Nitro Express,

nicknamed "elephant gun" for good reason,
double-barreled, with thumb-sized slugs
for dropping elephants, rhinos, cape buffalo

at full charge, as if they'd hit a concrete wall.
It fired two shots, all you'd get before you're
vulture nosh. What perfect unity of form

and bone-splintering function, barrel blue
as midnight, stock engraved with big game,
exotic as the Serengeti. It gave us our first rush

of a homegrown take on the Burkian sublime:
that throb exciting "the ideas of pain and danger."
You could bet your life on it. The Bible told us so.

ELEPHANT

We see him plod beneath a sequined girl
tossing kisses. Another day in harness,
lost in thought, it seems, the way his eyes

gaze out below the steep forehead. Does he think
of times in Chad or Togo, Mother showing
how to use his trunk to bathe with dust

or thrust through thorny copses, perhaps imparting
lore we can't be privy to? Or maybe
elephants don't remember well, don't even

think but simply try to stay alive
and breed. And yet that muted smile suggests
amusement, some wry plum we might not get

if he could tell us. But brighter hues beguile:
"Ah," we exclaim, forgetting all about him,
as the juggler sends up five batons aflame.

MOWING

I tell myself it's for the good, this grueling
roar around the yard to squelch it from
rebellion back to lawn, to get each blade

flush with the others for a perfect carpet,
as pictured on the Scotts bag. I do it
for the exercise and beauty. But could it

also serve the petty tyrant in me, who
wants the world to line up at attention,
ready for the white glove, detractions

to be neutralized, as with Stalin's railroad
across Siberia to nowhere, the Trans-Polar
Mainline, part of his Great Plan for the

Transformation of Nature, to be built by
"enemies of the people." 100,000 corpses
later, it's known as "The Dead Road."

Or Pharaoh's attempt to square the desert up
with giant plinths and pyramids built on
the backs of the usual square pegs. Or Hitler's

master plan for tidying his Aryan inner
landscape, those half-mile panoramas
of *sieg heils* erect and straight as bayonets,

those Auschwitz barracks neatly aligned.
"Mow them down," ordered General Vargas,
when striking workers for United Fruit

and their families assembled, after Mass,
in the main square of Ciénaga. An action
echoed at Baba Yar and the Katyn Forest,

at Wounded Knee and Sand Creek,
at Granada, Yangzhou, Batak, Nanking,
Hue, and My Lai. "Exterminate the brutes!"

cries Mr. Kurtz to his inner mower. "Yes,"
peeps a voice, as I watch a pair of rabbits
picnic on my freshly-clipped hibiscus.

SERENDIPITY

Said to be among the ten words
hardest to translate, it's what happened

when Fleming, forgetting to clean
his petri dish, discovered penicillin;

and Röntgen, fiddling with tubes
and gasses, hit on X-rays. Ditto

the stumbling onto corn flakes, matches,
superglue, vulcanized rubber, plastic,

Velcro, potato chips, stainless steel, popsicles,
microwave ovens, and Viagra. All serendipity.

It means the opposite of "Edsel," "winged tanks,"
"Sea Shoes," the "Vacuum Beauty Helmet";

of Midas' magic fingers, or the mantis male's
after-sex come-hug-me; or when, as a toddler,

I tried to feed the neighbor's Doberman,
a mild rehearsal for teen romance,

when, coaxed by hormones and the boogaloo,
I held my heart out to Melody Capone.

Walpole coined the term after reading a fairy tale
about three princes of "Serendip," now Sri Lanka.

So genteel and foreign-sounding, the word can
make us ransack memory, grab the Webster,

as we'd never need to do for "perfect storm,"
"Murphy's Law," or "clusterfuck."

ON THE ROAD AGAIN

Yes, can't wait,
like the trail gazers

selling their pine-board home
to board a Conestoga,

like Captains Cook
and Scott, drunk

on *terra incognita*
or Melville, signed on

for eighteen months
of open sea.

It's a chance, just a chance,
to ditch our old self,

its Raisin Bran normality,
its BarcaLounger comforts.

We just might miss
that turnoff to Sea World

or Mount Rushmore,
our reservations

at the Residence Inn.
Damn the electric bill,

the kids' college,
the annual checkup. Damn

time's winged ream job.
Damn the United Way.

Fire up the Explorer;
lay in some java,

Slim Jims, and a case
of Evil Eye. Flip

the radio to KISS
MYASS-FM. Next stop:

next stop, motherfuckers.

CAUTION:

Before using ladder,
be sure both ends
are secured against
something solid.

To climb down ladder,
reverse procedure
for climbing up.
If disorientation occurs,
stop and wait
till help arrives.
(To reduce waiting time
for help, call out, "Help.
Help. I'm on this ladder.")

Do not use ladder to provoke
oncoming motorists
or to attempt
to board their vehicles.

Avoid direct contact
with eyes.

**If experiencing low
self-esteem** or other anxiety
near ladder, say,

"Get back, you ladder,"
three times.

If ladder is found
in rectum,
contact physician
immediately.

ELISHA COOK, JR.

1903–1995

> *We've got to have a fall guy.*
> —Sam Spade

He's our kneecapped sap, punk chump
left holding humiliation's leaky bag,
the pouting patsy whose gat slips
his grip, hare-eyed gunsel who always

craps out at fortune's crooked table.
"Keep riding me, and they're gonna
be picking iron out of your liver,"
he warns Spade in *The Maltese Falcon*,

only to get trussed up with his own coat.
"You're a low-down lyin' Yankee," he calls
hired-gun Wilson in *Shane*, then draws
way too late. "If a guy's playin'

a hand, I let him play it," he, the stoolie,
says to Marlowe in *The Big Sleep*, before he's
forced to chug a toxic cocktail and spills
some cocked-up skinny. It's good

to see him stalk into quicksand or catch
a hot grenade, with his unstitched twitch,
his shifty-lipped little why-me routine,
this twerpy jerk who takes the rap for us.

THE HEREFORD WHEEL

Devised in Cincinnati, perfected in Chicago
to crown the city "hog butcher for the world,"
it resembled those huge wooden spools

used for heavy cable, but twice the size
and with five shackles chained to the action side,
where it hoisted hogs by a hind leg. It turned

slowly on the wall as chains clanked taut
and the hogs shrieked and flailed their way
up to the rail that sent them to be stuck,

scalded, de-haired, and butchered—Bosch
with sound effects, slaughter industrialized,
solution to payroll woes and wasted motion.

This disassembly line gave Ford the notion
to reverse it for assembling Model Ts
and Himmler to apply it to social engineering.

It's history now: the hogs are processed quietly,
gassed to sleep, moved on conveyer belts,
no more ugliness, no more human sounds.

III

LONG DISTANCE TO MY OLD COACH

The reception's not bad, across 50 years,
though his voice has lost its boot-camp timbre.
He's in his 80s now and, in a recent photo,

looks it, so bald and pale and hard to see
behind the tallowing of flesh. Posing with friends,
he's the only one who has to sit—the man

three of us couldn't pin. "The Hugger,"
they christened him before my class arrived—
for his bearlike shape and his first name, Hugh.

He fostered even us, the lowly track squad.
"Mr. Morrison," I still call him. "You were
the speedster on the team, a flash," he recalls

with a chuckle. That's where his memory of me
fades. And what have I retained of him beyond
the nickname, voice, and burly shape? The rest

could be invention: memory and desire's
sleight of hand as we call up those we think
we've known, to chat about the old days

and the weather, bum hips and cholesterol,
our small talk numbing as a dial tone,
serious as prayer.

LOOKING GOOD

In *Papillon*, Steve McQueen, who's been in solitary
six months in French Guiana, eating half-rations
and whatever bugs he finds, sticks his head out
of the slot in the wooden door and asks the prisoner
in the next cell, whose head is also out, "How
do I look?" "Good," lies the other guy who,
like McQueen, looks qualified for corpsedom.
"You, too," says McQueen.
                                    "You look good," we say
without the prompt, to the friend who's been on
chemo or the relative stowed in the memory ward
at Autumn House or Beacon Hill. "How do I look?"
I asked Mom before the eighth-grade dance, fumbling
with my cummerbund. "So very handsome,"
she said, ignoring the zit moonscape and braces
that gleamed like a Caddy bumper.
                                    "Do I look
OK?" the groom asked me at his shotgun wedding,
eyes bleary, brow dripping. "She always looks
so sweet," a neighbor said about Aunt Geraldine,
dressed for company, her blue hair freshly permed.
"It's a wonder," someone added after the viewing,
"how they make them look so good these days."

PEEK-A-BOO

You heard it in the crib, when from behind
the blanket, Dad startled you into giggles,
then vanished like Houdini. Years later,

he appeared in the bedroom mirror
looking out from your Harris Tweed
as you fixed your tie. The chill surged

like flu coming on, before you shook it off
and went down to greet the guests.
Later yet, if you should live so long,

Gramps' dead ringer may stare back
when you least expect—rheumy eyes,
tenuous flesh articulating brow and jaw.

That ancestral skull that's slept with you,
patient as a pallbearer all these years,
will touch your cheek: "Peek-a-Boo."

ELEGY

Myrna Loy's been stolen from her prime
years ago. You saw it in her ankles,
thick as pines, that nose—stripped by time

of their elegance and sweep. It's a crime
no punishment could stop, this troubling
of our star, spun off from her prime.

Must human beauty dwindle to a rind
tattooed with liver spots, scored with wrinkles?
Those ankles, those rheumy eyes. No charm

could save that face and figure, so sublime
they made the wily Dillinger less careful,
dreaming of her partnership in crime.

She played the perfect wife, the critics chimed
in chorus till they saw wattles dangling
beneath that smile, breath-stopping in its time.

Yet most of us grow old. We shouldn't pine
over one loss in a blight so universal.
But Myrna Loy's been stolen from her prime,
her cosy glamor grub for the glutton Time.

AFTER SURPRISING CONVERSIONS

They're aired between evening TV
sound bites of homicides, suicides,
fratricides, infanticides, fires, floods,

and pols. Befores, pajama-ed or in undies,
look old and lonely in their ills, one
with a headache big as her living room.

They buckle with pain, sneeze and cough
staccato, rush to the toilet, nod off
at their desks, snap at their worried spouses.

Afters jog together at Big Sur, cavort
with their now-adoring grandkids. Mates
hold hands in twin bathtubs, renewed

and busy at their sponsor-vetted
foreplay. A former wetter guffaws
worry-free at the Improv, while side effects—

dizziness, rash, fever, constipation,
incontinence, delusions. thrombosis, stroke—
slip by, all snickers and high-fives.

BACK TO WORK

The express line backs up
as the clerk keeps trying
to make the scanner
read the barcode
on a box of Tampax.
He's elderly, bespectacled,
s-shaped like someone
who spent his work life
bent above desk or bench
—making jewelry,
balances, footnotes.
His manner says
he's new here,
all squints and stiffness
as he drags the box
back and forth
across the screen,
guiding it as if wary
of a *tilt* sign,
laboring beneath
the looks we exchange.

Someone stalks off
to the next line over
as the box continues
back and forth. *Don*,
says the name tag,

which should say
Mr. Jacobson or
Professor Drake.
The Walmart vest
hangs like part
of a rented costume. *How*
May I Help You? it fawns.
At last, the scanner dings
and Don completes the bagging.
The line advances.

"Thank you," he says,
to the schoolgirl
as she huffs away,
his voice kindly
and dignified. "Thank you
for shopping here."

WINTER IN THE MALL

Striding in Adidases, shuffling in Florsheims,
they arrive before the shoppers, free from snow,
in couples, groups, or all alone. More time's
their goal, so, doing what their faith requires,
they undertake their pilgrimage, to and fro
among the Big Macs and the belted tires.

TO THE CIALIS LOVERS

What mortals or gods are these? O attic shape!
Fair attitude! With breed of bathtub-seated man
and maiden near-o'erwrought among a span
of oaks or near the ocean. Bold lovers, napes
and thighs are out; but holding hands may reap
some hay. Cold pastoral with separate ceramics
warmed by ardor and tadalafil, tidy as Saran,
set to sail the Merlot-dark sea or L.L. Beanscape.

When old age hath this generation blurred,
you—or your replacements—shall still beard woe
and its gloomy offspring. O friend of humankind
to whom you say, "Beauty's for the birds,
and Truth has toodled south not far behind—
that's all we know on earth or care to know."

OLD FOOLS

Don't believe them
that they used to dance
a mean foxtrot.
They've always been
this way: doddering
with canes and walkers,
slowing traffic,
wattles swaying as they
wheeze into view,
wobbly as drunks in fog,
shamelessly wasting
space in lines
and parking lots.

Imagine going
out in public
looking like that.
And those noises and
odors. *Pardon me,*
they flash at us
like a note from the Pope.
Pass the Air Wick.

Mutter this
and rasp that.
Don't get them
started on how lousy

everything's turned
since Kennedy won
and men quit
wearing hats.

Why don't they stick
to their own kind?
We don't have time
to deal with these people.

"Drop dead,"
we'd like to tell them,
which seems the one thing
they're halfway good at.

WORSE THAN USELESS

Maybe you said that about a piece of crap
you bought online or what advertised itself
as "customer service." Maybe a coach
said it when you missed an easy tackle

or some boss muttered it on your first day,
when you cooked the curly fries too long.
Maybe you even said it to yourself, though
you didn't really mean it, not then anyway.

But what about those stored in "total care"
facilities, named for dying things or seasons:
sunset, autumn, golden fields; or for fantasies
like Bel-air Manor and Sunshine Vista. What

can their inmates call themselves, nodding off
or watching out their solitary window,
which overlooks the parking lot, hoping
to spot someone they know or maybe just

a cardinal or finch flitting by, instead of
the scrounging sparrows, all of whom still
have some function in the scheme of things?
The body's built to atrophy. Its organs clog

or slowly peter out, despite the ads that make believe it can't be true. Lay up your poison pills, your .45, before you can't remember where you get them or which orifice to put them in.

Make yourself useful.

FAST FORWARD

We are such stuff that dreams are made on . . .
    —Prospero

At our reunion lunch, the wall calendar
starts to flip—May 1959, August 1965,
June 2014—like in those corny movies,
where young folks suddenly find themselves
doddering down Cemetery Lane. No,
the years spin like on that dial in Wells'
time machine, but we're stuck outside,
exposed in short sleeves and Bermudas,
pickled down by decades of time's
radiation, soon to be all chicken skin
and blotches. No, it's that time-lapse
shrivel when Dracula parties past vault time,
ass dwindling, locks gone wispy white.
No, it's some lad in an amnesia flick,
bludgeoned for his small change,
who wakes to strangers talking
prostates, colonoscopies, living wills. No,
it's the Wicked Witch, her immortality
doused by a child who's dreamed her.
What a world, classmates, what a world.

FALLING

"I've fallen, and I can't get up," a granny
cries on a TV ad that's now a punch line.
"Fall in," barks the Gunny to his grunts,
who know they've fallen on hard times.
Winter's near, we think, as leaves whisper
"fall" and poets fall to writing odes.

We mourn the fallen as our anthem plays.
"I will fall upon them like a bear robbed
of her cubs," says *Hosea 3:8*. "In Adam's
fall, we sinned all," expounds the preacher
as we fall asleep in our pew. We'd rather fall
in love, though that can lead to a falling-out.

Falling short of oxygen or blood can lead to
falling dead. Caesar had the falling sickness;
his death fell on the ides of March, after which
a fall befell the Empire. With so much falling,
our fallen world wastes no pity, falling through
space, on a downed old lady's sorry case.

YA KNOW?

It's been one of those days
when the pot calls the kettle Duane,

when the knuckles of contumely
rap the forehead of resolve,

and the weeds of crime strangle
the begonias of ebullience,

when the morning pills scatter
like roaches under light,

when the PC, jammed in sleep mode,
dreams it's a machine gun,

and Customer Service advises
what sounds like "Die, Terpsichore cootie!"

when *Weltschmerz* gets the will
in another hammerlock,

when the starter chortles "nyuk, nyuk, nyuk,"
and AAA plays you a selection of Yani,

and an earworm keeps replaying
the Yani on its amplified banjo.

MiraLAX®

The license plate
of the babe in the TV ad
reads, *I ♥ my lax.*

She's an actress,
but where the aged
are housed, the thought

of miracles can trickle
down to those produced
by pills and ointments.

Alone in their room,
by the only window, some
love their laxative,

more than they might
a feast of loaves and fishes,
for which they've lost

their taste. For some,
it's their only comforter,
who never stays long.

YOU AND YOUR SHADOW

Shadow loves the little children, the way they
  lie propped on their silky pillows,
  quiet as daguerreotypes.

Shadow loves the grown-ups, too—how,
  when he drops them in the dark water, they relax,
  al dente.

Call him workaholic, though sometimes he'll
  pop open a can of sorrow to kick back and pull out
  a program from his morgue of old TV shows.

Shadow's favorite TV star is Mr. Jimmy "Schnozzola"
  Durante, whose nose casts a big banana shadow
  when he flashes his profile and says, "Hot-cha-cha!"

Durante knocks 'em dead with his string-backed
  finale, "Me and My Shadow." Schnozzola and, rising
  behind him, Schnozzola-No-More.

Then there's *Gomer Pyle, USMC*. Shadow weeps
  sometimes, knowing the dead Marines can
  always use a few good shadows. *Semper Mortuus.*

Shadow was born blind, which is why you
  have to catch your breath when he holds tight.
  To find you, he depends on Umbra, his seeing-eye.

Even so, Shadow loves a good joke, like why
the Shadow crossed the road. (To keep tabs
on all his little fryers. Hot-cha-cha!)

LAST WORDS

If only for those you leave behind,
don't be forced to cram and get cut short,
like poor Max Baer, who noted, "Here
I go," or Pancho Villa, pleading "Don't let it
end like this. Tell them I said something."
Ibsen, hearing friends outside his room
agree that he seemed much better,
had only time to sit up and announce,
"On the contrary!" then drop dead.

Beware the blindside, or you may depart
like William Barton Rogers, stopped midway
through his commencement speech at
"bituminous coal" or Dylan Thomas,
telling his White Horse Tavern buddies,
"I've had eighteen straight whiskeys.
I think that's the record" or Union General
John Sedgwick, confident, "They couldn't
hit an elephant at this distance."

If you favor wit, you're up against pros
like Heine, who said, as worried friends
pressed around, "God will forgive me:
it's his *métier*." Voltaire, when asked by priests
to forswear Satan, countered, "This is no time
to make new enemies." The grand Pavlova
quipped, "Get my swan costume ready."

If high sentence is your choice, there's always
John Q. Adams' "This is the last of earth.
I am content." Or, in certain situations,
Patrick Henry's "Give me liberty
or give me death," though some say
he followed up with, "Let me rephrase that."

Or perhaps you'd simply like to underscore
the world's injustice, like Thomas Grasso,
who strangled one aged victim with her
Christmas lights, and said, about his last meal:
"I didn't get my SpaghettiOs. I got spaghetti.
I want the press to know that."

WHAT A DRAG IT IS GETTING OLD

In street clothes,
sans platinum mane,
ex-rock-god David Lee Roth
looks a head shorter,
his wiseass grin gone jittery
as a cornered pickpocket's.
He's pitching a new, bluegrass
version of "Jump." In the video,
his Nureyev leap's faded
to a few obligatory kicks
before a hapless band
in a number that might do
to open a Sam's or Costco.

It's Borg trying for a comeback
with his wooden racket,
Nader running again,
Keaton after the talkies
came to stay. It's the old
story, which flops on
the sofa and, after putting
up its dogs, never tires
of boring us to death.

STICKY NOTES

They tell us to pay the bills, water
the begonias, wish Aunt Estelle
(the old bat) a happy 86th.
Our need accrues as years go by
and memory totters. We slap them
on the fridge, car keys, toothbrush,
though sometimes we can't tell
what the hell we wrote on them.

Near the final chill, we stick them
on birds and trees—*goldfinch,*
chickadee, sugar maple, weeping
birch—but they come unstuck,
swirl away, muddled among
the snow geese and brown leaves.

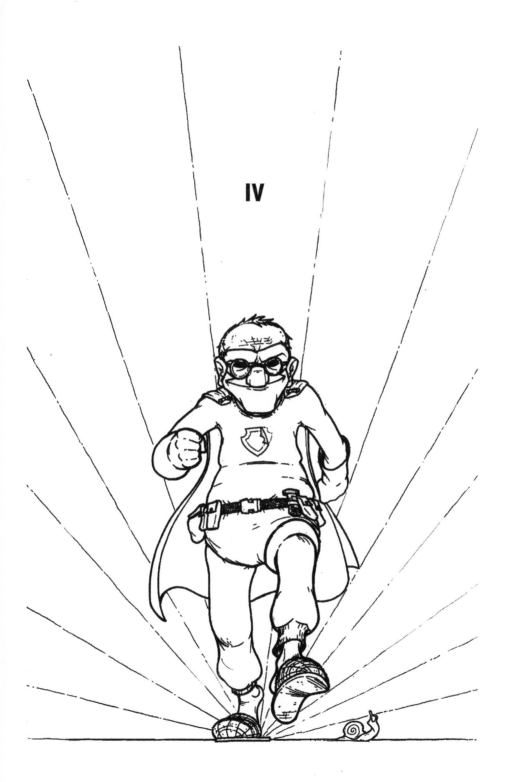

IV

OLDGUY: SUPERHERO

feels like a young guy in a bad costume.
The arms and legs sag, and the waist's
too tight. Where there should be a large *S*,
golden star, or lightning bolt, there's what
looks like a zero, and on his trunks, *Depend*.

The boots look more like flannel slippers.
Some lout's made off with his super-hearing
and X-ray vision, leaving only an Ampli Ear
and Coke-bottle lenses. Like certain sheep,
he doesn't fly so much as plummet. He hasn't

smashed through a good wall or door
since before he can remember, which is
a little after breakfast. Speeding bullets
and tall buildings must now be turtles
and molehills. He has no fear

of an erection lasting more than four hours,
but he's depressed and often flatulent.
His best tactic, the long wait, accounts
for the demise of many a foe, that
or rambling on and on and on and on,

which can paralyze from as far as ten feet.
He's not handsome like Clark Kent or rich
like Bruce Wayne, but in the prolonged run
he can be a deadly opponent, if he doesn't
mix you up with someone else.

OLDGUY: SUPERHERO, COUNTERTERRORIST

Oldguy's in line for his Social Security check
when a man enters carrying a gun and wearing

a suicide vest. Though people start to scream,
Oldguy continues dog-paddling through

the shallows of his memory, till the terrorist,
noticing his scarlet cape and blank expression,

shoves the gun in his face and asks how it feels
to face certain death. "Same as usual,"

says Oldguy, mistaking the threat for a rare
show of interest, which prompts him to dust off

his five examples why everything's gone
to goddamn hell since Truman fired Custer.

After a while, the terrorist's eyelids droop,
and he slumps into a nearby chair, snoring.

When the gun drops to the floor, Oldguy politely
retrieves it, just as the SWAT team bursts in.

"How did you do it, Oldguy?" asks the press.
"Glue what?" he says.

OLDGUY: SUPERHERO, TOP ELIMINATOR

Oldguy goes looking for adventure
in the Oldguymobile, a refurbished
Oscar Mayer Wienermobile acquired
by agreeing to take it off the former
owner's hands. He's repainted it

Marine green, with lightning bolts
that wobble across the wiener's sides.
The horn, when it works, plays what
sounds like a kazoo-band version of
"I Wish I Were an Oscar Mayer Wiener."

Sadly, the helmet Oldguy mounted
on the wiener's front end makes it
resemble a half-erect penis. Unfazed
by the ensuing catcalls, Oldguy guns
his engine as he and a Stingray guy

pull up to a red light. He remembers
driving the Younguymobile, 426 Hemi,
supercharged, chopped, and Frenched,
ground quaker, babe waker, heartbreaker
to all takers. When the light flashes green,

he spills hot thermos coffee down his crotch,
causing him to swerve into the Stingray,
which accelerates into a sewage truck.
"Feel lucky now, punk?" says Oldguy,
lurching on his horn's melodious lilt.

OLDGUY: SUPERHERO
ON WATCH

Oldguy gets bored
watching *Flipper* reruns

on his set's only channel
in his secret headquarters

above Nu-Day Loans.
He decides he'll go out

to check for malfeasance.
But things on the street

seem pretty routine—
people hurrying past,

eyeing his costume
with a mix of pity

and trepidation, a gaggle
of teens sneering, "Up,

up, and am-scray, Grandpa!"
as he spots an antique

Packard parked by a meter
that reads *Expired*.

"Too late again," he sighs,
thinking the sign applies

to the missing driver. "Done in
by some gang of truants?"

Crestfallen, he returns
to headquarters, where

"Flipper and the Puppy"
is kicking off another

24-hour marathon.
Oldguy can't recall

whether that's the one
where Flipper saves

the puppy from sharks
or his favorite, where Flipper rises,

T-Rex-on-steroids-size,
out of the sea to terrorize

a coastal town, making wiseass
beach punks run for Mama.

OLDGUY: SUPERHERO—
HIS UTILITY BELT

One inflatable five-man-tent capsule,
   Italian army surplus.

One pair mini long-range spotter glasses,
   right lens missing.

One telescoping blowpipe,
   slightly bent.

Ten curare-tipped blowpipe darts,
   [use by 1/1/56].

One pair bat-shaped handcuffs,
   delivered to wrong address.

One Party Animal joy buzzer,
   for enemy banquet infiltration.

One ultra-sheer camouflage net,
   wherever it is.

Four Hershey bars, with almonds,
   for urchin recruitment.

One Ejector Model Baby Hammerless Revolver,
   1929 Johnson Smith model.

Twin Beta X-22 Kinetic Gizmoids,
   set on recharge.

One Big Cat rupture truss,
   new condition.

One denture grapple, for eaves, napes,
   or crotches.

Four tear-gas suppositories, for last-resort
   escapes.

OLDGUY: SUPERHERO, HOMIE

Oldguy's on his way to the convenience store
for a beer and a Slim Jim but takes the wrong

street and winds up in the barrio, where he's
spotted by a carload of lowriders, who buck

the car over the curb at him, stopping an inch
away. Oldguy's mind's strayed back to when

he could piss his name in dry concrete,
but his blank stare is taken as mad-dogging.

The lowriders admire his big cojones and decide
to make him a member. They give him a jacket,

black leather, their name blood-red on the back—
The Latin Assassins—with room for his moniker

underneath. They christen him *El Anciano* and try
to teach him their hand sign, but his shaky version

looks like the finger. They stare as he wanders off.
"See that finger, man?" says the leader, turning

to the others. "Don't fuck with that guy: he
don't give a shit." Soon a cop stops Oldguy

and asks where he thinks his fucking gang ass
is going. Oldguy understands this as a request

for his new gang sign. After he flashes it,
a nurse says, "Try to drink this." But as he heals,

word of Oldguy's ballsy gesture to the system
feeds the legend of *El Anciano, Fist of Fire*.

OLDGUY: SUPERHERO
VS. HIS NEMESIS

Here comes Death again, sickle in one hand,
portable chess set in the other. "How 'bout
we have a nice game," he asks Oldguy—"nice"

because he keeps an extra queen up each
rancid sleeve. Oldguy, who was napping,
pretends he's still asleep. Death acts concerned,

tells him he should get more exercise, expand
his interests, take up cliff diving, bomb disposal,
Russian roulette. Oldguy, who once could defuse

cluster bombs in mid-dive, farts and rolls over,
goes back to dreaming of the days when
he used his X-ray vision on bras and panties

and Death seemed as harmless as that little creep
in fifth grade, sole and sulky member of the chess club.
My mistake, thinks Oldguy, *but he* is *a creep.*

Ever flighty, Death gathers up his chess set
and zips off to topple a Planned Parenthood clinic
onto its occupants. He's a right-to-lifer.

But it's past closing time: no one's there. Death,
now a dozen victims behind his daily quota,
curses Oldguy, dreams of retiring to Forest Lawn,

where other notables rest beneath the hyacinths
and greenswards, where silence *is* golden,
peace silver. "That's the fuckin' life," he sighs.

OLDGUY: SUPERHERO
BROODS ON UNWANTED HAIR

Oldguy notices the hair that used to
grow on his head now thrusts out
of his ears and nose so thickly that
he's had to buy an electric trimmer
from The Shopping Channel, which
turned out to be a piece of crap.

He's heard that, after you die, your hair
keeps growing. He shudders to think
of the coffin filling up with hair, which,
like the Blob, then forces itself out
under the lid and up toward light
till it makes a hedge around his grave.

He wonders if this growth could be
the start of reincarnation. Will he
come back as an orangutan, wooly
worm—or, better, a 21st-century
Cavalier? With locks flowing from
the right place again, he'd battle

the Roundheads, who seem to be
taking over everything. He'd fine them
for skullduggery, bounce pool cues
off their billiard pates, stick wombats
down their undies, flies in their ointment.
He'd gag them with big wild-hairballs.

OLDGUY: SUPERHERO,
STEADY HAND

When Oldguy spots an old lady waiting
for the light to change, he steps up
and gently takes her arm. On green, he

helps her off the curb and into the street,
remembering his Boy Scout days, when
he earned all the merit badges in a day

and invented some new ones: Missile
Interception, Boulder Shattering, Volcano
Stoppering, Elephant Bench-Pressing.

All the Girl Scouts wanted to camp out
with him, stitch up a lanyard or two,
explore the more advanced knots, but

the red phone clamored all the time:
off he'd go to thwart the latest megalomaniac
or suck the air from another hurricane.

He needed a silo to hold his medals. Now,
after he gets the old lady across, she pats
his hand and asks, "Do you need more help?"

OLDGUY: SUPERHERO
UNDERCOVER

On patrol in the city one evening, Oldguy
stops to relieve himself on an out-of-the-way
shrub, which is actually an in-the-way

poodle being walked by a local matron,
who immediately summons the police.
Arrested for indecent exposure, Oldguy

thinks he's to infiltrate the "indecent" other
occupants in the police van and "expose" any
upcoming plots. To gain their confidence,

he says he's "iced" a Meals-on-Wheels lady.
They report this to the officers in front, hoping
to earn reduced sentences. Locked up,

in max-security, Oldguy confides to a janitor
he mistakes for a uniformed contact that he's
in with the indecents, that the *go* signal

will be two longs and a short. The janitor
contacts the city paper, informing them
the police are mistreating a harmless old

looney. To prevent a PR disaster, the chief
has the charges dismissed and, as cameras
flash, presents Oldguy with a gold plaque

naming him a *Senior Posse Member*.
In the front-page photo, Oldguy can be seen
sizing up a shrub-shaped floral display.

OLDGUY: SUPERHERO—
HIS ORIGIN

Oldguy's from Smallville, just like Superman,
who got all the press. But Oldguy was born there,
off Elm Street, where he was christened "Irving. "

His parents, common as lima beans, chose
to ignore his flying around the nursery and his
solving the calculus problem at three months.

But the neighbors complained about him riding
their kids on his back when he soared for ice cream,
rattling their windows and spooking their pets.

So he was packed off to boarding school, where
thanks to a wise mentor and loose regulations,
he matured into Youngguy: Superhero—

though low profile, discreet. Who tipped the balance
against the Nazis? Pump primed the U. N.?
Rid the world of polio and Stalin? Neutralized

Pol Pot and the KKK? "Mum" was his only motto.
Then one day, he got up, looked in the mirror,
and suddenly   Oldguy stared back.

OLDGUY: SUPERHERO, ASSOCIATE

Oldguy gets a job as a greeter at Walmart,
where he wears a blue vest with *How May
I Help You?* on the back and a smiley-face
button on the front. If things go well, he can
add a gold-star pin with *Management*

Appreciates ME! across it, or a comet
pin with *Awesome Job!* on its tail. But
most customers don't want to be greeted;
some balk at having even strangers see them
shopping there. One woman smacks him

with her purse. So he tones it down to
a nod and a wink, but a burly guy thinks
he's touting blowjobs and shoves him
into a DVD display. Oldguy, to keep
his identity secret, opts not to strip

to his superhero garb. He finds greeting
to be harder than it was to stop Rodan
from flash-frying Dubuque. When he tries
just to look good-natured, management
decides he's become a liability, another

worthless senior trying to take advantage
of an American job provider. To get him
out, guards take each arm and, grinning,
tell him he's going to meet Mr. Walmart.
It's turned cold, and the raindrops sting.

OLDGUY: SUPERHERO ATTENDS THE
ASSOCIATED SUPERHEROES CONFERENCE

Oldguy signed up late, so he has to share a room
at the Lone Star Motel, which charges by the hour,

with Repulsiveguy, who drives villains away
with his nose-blow rendition of "Danke Schoen,"

and his fart-take on "Bubbles in the Wine." Oldguy
leaves early for the conference, at the Downtown

Hubris. He hopes to network a little, compare
notes with Superman, Captain Marvel, Batman,

who have fancy booths in the big hall, where they
sign autographs and talk down to admirers.

He has to stand in line, where he's jostled by
a desperate army of wannabes, one of whom

snarls, "Keep it moving, Grandpa." Oldguy
might have used his denture grapple on the kid

if it weren't soaking back at the hotel. When he
gets to the front of the line, Superman scribbles

an autograph on Oldguy's utility belt and,
when Oldguy tries to start a conversation, snaps,

"Move it along, Gramps." Oldguy then attends
a panel, where Wonder Woman, the Hulk,

Captain America, and Aquaman float around
the room on their notoriety. Later, Oldguy's

turned away from the hospitality room for
lack of insider credentials. By this time, he

needs a nap, so he walks back to the Lone Star,
where Repulsiveguy has driven off even the pimps

and junkies with his projectile-vomiting routine.
Things seem so bleak that Oldguy and he go out

for a drink with Daylateguy and Kickmeguy.
At the Jungle Room, after a fifth Pink Volcano,

they discover how much they have in common,
harmonize on several choruses of "Danke Schoen."

McOLDGUY: SUPERHERO

Oldguy's assigned to Window One, where
orders and payment are taken. A woman
in a giant SUV filled with children rattles off
her order faster than Oldguy can get it

onto the touch screen. When he asks her
to repeat and she starts huffing through the list,
a man behind her blares his horn repeatedly,
and the other people in line take sides for

or against him. The increasing commotion
brings the manager to Oldguy's post. He says
this isn't the first time Oldguy's disrupted
a system required to prevail in the struggle

between Ronald and that red-headed hippie
Wendy and her ilk. When Oldguy reminds him
those characters aren't real, the manager says
they're more real than some old fart taking up

space in the business world. Oldguy's again
tempted to reveal his true identity, perhaps
this time with a zap from his pocket defibrillator.
But the manager's already out oozing apologies

to the SUV woman and the honker. Oldguy
supersizes a *fuck-you* and three *bite-me*'s,
with secret sauce, onto the special-order screen
before he backfires off in the Oldguymobile.

OLDGUY: SUPERHERO
DISCOVERS HIS BROTHER

Oldguy, known to some as Oldwhiteguy,
discovers that Oldblackguy lives next door.
After getting acquainted, they go out for
a couple of beers at a local bar, where it

dawns on them that, though Youngwhiteguy
got all the breaks, now, as oldguys they're
treated as equals: better off dead. In light
of this, they celebrate how racial slurs now

seem innocuous as Nerf balls. "Kneel and
lick my boot," opens Oldwhiteguy. "Bow and
kiss my black ass," counters Oldblackguy. "Coon,"
shouts one. "Ofay," retorts the other, followed

by tearful laughter. After a while, the regulars
complain to the bartender about the oldguys,
who ought to be locked up in some home,
acting like they owned the place. A bouncer

escorts them out through an alley door and
shoves them into a pile of uncollected trash.
After helping each other up, they head for
the nearest liquor store. "Another fine mess

you got us into, Brillo pad," grins one. "Me
and yo momma's dried-up titties, bird shit,"
chuckles the other as they persevere, ambling
as if they owned the whole damned street.

Biographical Note

Former Poet Laureate of Missouri, William Trowbridge is the author of seven full poetry collections and four chapbooks. His awards include an Academy of American Poets Prize, a Pushcart Prize, a Bread Loaf Writers' Conference scholarship, a Camber Press Poetry Chapbook Award, and fellowships from The MacDowell Colony, Ragdale, Yaddo, and The Anderson Center. He teaches in the University of Nebraska at Omaha low-residency MFA in Writing Program and lives in the Kansas City area.